STEAMPUNK FASHION

Spurgeon Vaughn Ratcliffe

GRAFFITO

STEAMPUNK FASHION

Art Direction by Samuel Ratcliffe.

Published in 2012 by Graffito Books Ltd, 32 Great Sutton Street, London EC1V 0NB, UK
www.graffbooks.co.uk
© Graffito Books Ltd, 2012.
ISBN 978-0956028-44-0

British Library cataloguing-in-publication data:
A catalogue record of this book is available at the British Library.

Printed in China.

CONTENTS

FOREWORD

Tom Banwell...8

Dr. Brassy Steamington...20

J-Chan Designs...30

Robert Dancik...36

Dasowl...42

Gaia Noir...46

Gryphon's Egg...50

Friston Ho'okano...54

Impero London...60

KMK Designs...70

Lady Love Lloyd...74

Legendary Costume Works...78

Lost Legends...86

Mechanical Mirage...92

Ms Vontoon...100

Octopus Me...106

Purpuratum...114

Skinz 'N' Hydez...124

Steampunk Couture...130

Steampunk Overlord...142

Thin Gypsy Thief...148

APPENDIX

FOREWORD

A TRUE ACCOUNT OF THE WORLD OF STEAMPUNK FASHION AS PENNED BY SPURGEON VAUGHN RATCLIFFE

Running along the flagstones of Jermyn Street one sunny morning, a few months ago, I paused momentarily to check my pocketwatch. By happy coincidence my eye was distracted by the sight of the jewel-like Princes Arcade, whence stood a shop of the most uncharacteristic beauty. Above a window display of complex leatherwork and flowing regalia read a sign: Impero London. Intrigued I strode forth and entered. Once inside I had the pleasure of meeting the talented proprietors, Tilly and Mumtaz. Over a cup of freshly brewed tea, the two designers were only too pleased to tell me about the recently-hatched movement that is Steampunk. I found myself overjoyed and enraptured by the secret energy of this wonderful world of creative genii. With a flourish I took out my quill and notebook, penning, though then I knew it not, the first notes of a new book I would offer to connoisseurs of the extraordinary everywhere, *Steampunk Fashion.*

I left Impero a new man, with new purpose: I was going to make myself known to the world of Steampunk fashionistas! Excited at the prospect of collating a compendium that encompassed the breadth of Steampunk styles (and an international adventure), I looked round to ensure everyone was otherwise distracted, and leapt into one of my many London travelling devices, the Eros fountain in Piccadilly Circus. Carried on an instant stream of subterranean ether, I emerged from the Kilauea Volcano in Hawaii. 'Twas there I met with the master of Hawaiian floristry come Steampunk Jeweler, Friston Ho'okano. And it was from this magical island that I donned my deep sea diving gear and trekked some 10,000 miles across the bottom of the Ocean, and then a further 3,000 miles over the ancient mountains of Peru, from thence to travel deep into the Brazilian rainforest. My mission was clear – to meet with biotechnologician/explorer Larissa Haut of Purpuratum. After an intense induction in high-style and intellect combined, and with new found knowledge of Steampunk's love of true, unsullied nature, I swallowed a concoction of stimulants from the sap of that extraordinary jungle creeper, *Bulleyus Bulleyallis,* in order that I might find the strength to man the rudders of a gigantic airship that was to propel me towards that part of the Americas that lies north of the Equator.

This remarkable, and in many ways still uncharted, territory proved a rich land indeed and it was here that I encountered.......the renowned international Steampunk exhibitor Tom Banwell; the winged lord of Steampunk finery, Kyle Miller of Thin Gypsy Thief; the prolific Kato of Steampunk Couture; the queen of brass, Kimberlee Turner a.k.a Dr. Brassy Steamington; the visionary stylist and artisan, Jessica Rowell of J-Chan Designs; fetishist of the found object Robert Dancik; tailors of circus stardom, Deborah S. Sciales and Oliver W. Lowe of DASOWL; the grimly comic mask maker Shawn Darling, of Gryphon's Egg; textile sculptresses, Sheridyn and Kaitlyn McClain of KMK Designs; masters of disguise Amy and Brayton Carpenter of Legendary Costume Works; celebrity steampunk armorer Skinz N Hydez and lastly, but not in the least least, the deep sea Jeweler Deana Fukatsu, of Octopus Me.

Though exhausted and my mind dizzy with phantasmagorical designs, I still had enough might to assemble a transportation device that vaporized me into the virtual, pixel universe of Kazuhiko Nakamura of Mechanical Mirage, whose digital visions have inspired Steampunk fashion designers the world over. With my trusty time machine intact I beamed myself from Kazuhiko's native Japan to the Scottish Highlands, where, atop a craggy hillside, I discussed the merits of recycled materials with gothic Steampunk designer Jane Faye, of Gaia Noir. To my delight, the creator of militarised Steampunk insignia, Ms Vontoon, appeared also, and presented to me equipment that would ease the last legs of my journey. From this highland mount I had a marvelous vantage point from whence to launch my one man flying contraption that, with the benefit of a strong wind and some elbow grease, took me all the way to Brittany, France, where I delighted in the opulent gowns of Lady Love Lloyd, and thence, having heard much talk of the fantastical Marco Ribbe and Sina Collins of Lost Legends, to Heilbronn, in the newly unified land of Germania.

A surfeit of inspiration and explosive creativity made me relish the thought of pausing to set my thoughts to parchment. It wasn't long before I, Spurgeon Vaughn Ratcliffe, found myself in a draughty attic room, forgotten by time, in the city of Berlin. Here I lovingly unfurled my notes, photographs and graphic drawings to start the painstaking process of inputting them, via my ethereal-electrical thought-wave pith helmet into my Portable Document Fermenting device. Some eleven months later, with sacks of coal and barrels of Reichenbach Falls water consumed, you now hold the result in your, I hope begloved, hands. As you turn the pages I trust you will feel some of the wonder, amazement and elemental joy that I felt when first encountering the evidential artistry of man's creative spirit as herein revealed.

Based in a small rural town in the foothills of the Sierra Nevada, northern California, Tom Banwell came to Steampunk in circuitous fashion. "As a child I had a fascination with helmets and other hats and I started building a collection." With no formal training in art or fashion, Tom stumbled into a job at Lake Tahoe, making belts, purses and sandals. "That was 1972; four years later I decided to combine my new skills with my hat fascination and started a business making Western leather hats." These he sold all over the USA and the business was enough

of a success that he was able to sell it. There followed another period of dabbling. "I was messing around with woodcarving and then learnt to cast in resin, which turned into another business, casting figurines, imitating materials such as bronze, wood and marble." He didn't know it then, but these skills were to prove useful. One day, in 2008, surfing Etsy, he came across Steampunk as a design genre. He was hooked, and returned

to his first love, leather-working, and created his iconic plague mask. This became a Steampunk hit and since then Tom hasn't stopped. "I now use those resin skills in my work. Steampunk has endless aesthetic possibilities; I find just within mask-making there's massive room for creative expression. I love to work leather in new directions, to dream up new characters, and am amazed at the constant evolution of shapes and colours. It's the ability of Steampunk fashion to transform the wearer that remains an endless source of fascination to me."

LEFT AND ABOVE:
Dr. Beulenpest, Steampunk Plague Doctor with Plague Doctor Mask, Top grain vegetable-tanned leather, cold-cast aluminium eyepieces and beak, steel dome rivets, tinted lenses.

LEFT: *Steampunk Horned Helmet With Respirator*, Oak-tanned leather, brass studs and rivets, domed brass respirator pieces.
ABOVE: *Pachydermos Steampunk Gas Mask*. Vegetable-tanned leather, brass rivets, copper ear-pieces.

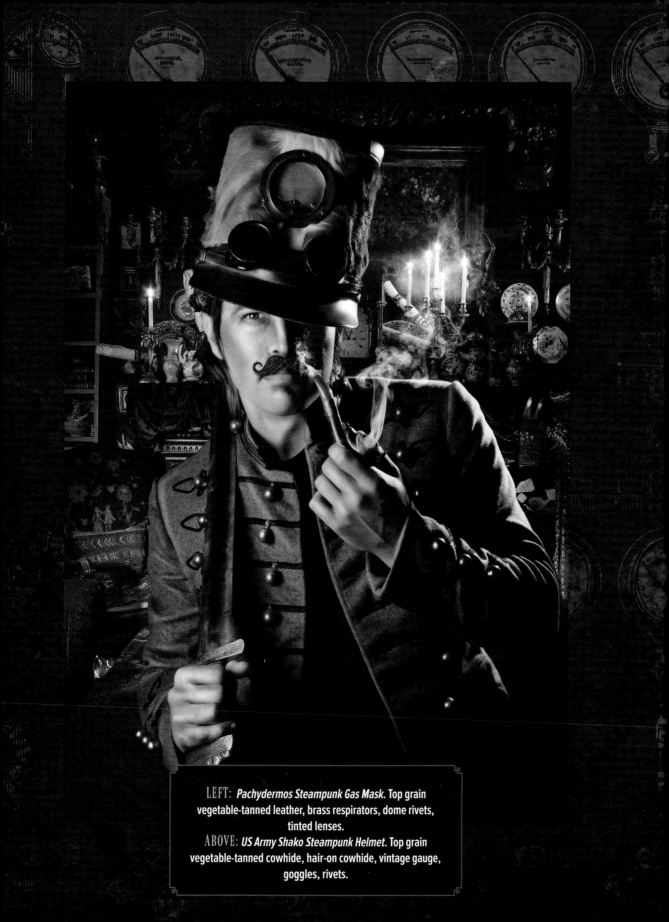

LEFT: *Pachydermos Steampunk Gas Mask.* Top grain vegetable-tanned leather, brass respirators, dome rivets, tinted lenses.

ABOVE: *US Army Shako Steampunk Helmet.* Top grain vegetable-tanned cowhide, hair-on cowhide, vintage gauge, goggles, rivets.

LEFT: *Ichabod Plague Doctors' Masks.* White and black vegetable-tanned leather, cold-cast aluminium, rivets.

ABOVE: *Ragnarok Industrial Strength Gas Masks Emerging From the Burrow.* Vegetable-tanned leather, cold-cast aluminium fittings, rusty respirators.

ABOVE LEFT: *Steampunk Helmet.* Vegetable-tanned leather, brass and steel fittings, textile-covered hose.

LEFT: *Ragnarok Steampunk Gas Mask (variation).* Vegetable-tanned leather, cold-cast aluminium fittings and domed aluminium cages.

ABOVE: *Airship Captain With Excursionist Leather Respirator.* Vegetable-tanned leather, resin canisters, rivets and button studs.

LEFT: *Sentinel with Defender Steampunk Gas Mask and Helmet.* Handmade vegetable-tanned cowhide, cold-cast metal fittings, 'sea anemone' respirators, Gryphon plate and lamp, charcoal lenses.

ABOVE: *Victorian Dandy with Red Steampunk Gas Mask.* Handmade vegetable-tanned cowhide, cold-cast metal fittings, resin and brass screws.

"I started doing my art in 1986. In those days it was really hard to explain my vision: the 'Steampunk' term, which defines it perfectly, hadn't been invented," says Dr Brassy a.k.a Kimberlee Turner. She decribes her creative process as "like breathing...totally organic. It's totally fabulous the way the whole Steampunk genre has exploded in the past year." Dr Brassy has many sources of inspiration, from hardware stores and her 1904 Singer sewing machine, to low budget vintage science fiction movies. Amongst contemporary artists she cites Harry Wood of Oscarcrow Designs – "he helped me embrace metalworking" – , Jill Lawrence of Twistedsisterarts and Brenda Sue Lansdowne of Bsueboutiques. Dr Brassy is steeped in the Steampunk scene. She is a contributor to Steampunk Lab, Steampunk Empire and is involved in the music scene (Time Lord, Jon Magnificent is a close friend). She has also appeared as a brain-eating zombie in *The League of S.T.E.A.M.* webisodes. When the urge to create grabs her "it comes in waves. When that wave hits I go into the studio and become a mad scientist for a day. I also have dry spells when I stare at my desk and nothing comes out." Dr Brassy receives commissions from all over the world; her work has been shown by the Museum of Monterrey, CA and at the MYTH masque in Hollywood.

LEFT: *Antebellum Steamer's Garden Necklace.* Sterling silver over brass.
RIGHT: *Midnight Flight Hat Pin.* Sterling silver over brass.

LEFT: *Clockwork No 7 and Clockwork No 9 Necklaces*. Brass and steel.
ABOVE: *Aeronaut Feathers Necklace*. Brass.

ABOVE: *Midnight Flight Necklace*. Sterling silver over brass; Swarovski jet crystal.
RIGHT: *Airship Horizons Cuff*. Copper over brass.

ABOVE: *Sparrow Compass Choker.* Brass and pearls with celluloid.
RIGHT, CLOCKWISE FROM TOP LEFT: *Clockworx Suspension Earrings,* brass and ice; *Hovercraft in Filligree II,* brass and ice; *Theatrical Luminosity Top Hat,* brass leather and silk.

ABOVE, CLOCKWISE FROM TOP LEFT: *Sightmares™ Steampunk Eye Necklaces: Solar Flare, La Grenouille, Time Master, Blood Moon*. Brass, glass and leather.
RIGHT: *Sightmares™ T-Rex Eye Necklace*. Brass, glass and leather.

"I first started doing costume design in about 2008; it was at the *Au* event in Dallas, the same year that I attended a Steampunk panel, and I was captivated", says Jessica Rowell (a.k.a. J-Chan Designs). In particular Jessica remembers a rusted backpack worn by the panel hostess and a baby stroller with brass pipes, coils and gears. Fascination turned to disappointment, as so many designers jumped onto the band-wagon, with hugely cliched pieces. "It wasn't until 2011 that I created Steampunk pieces that I was truly proud of; I had made a decision that I would only work in the genre if I could bring something new to the table, which led me to combining Steampunk with Greek mythology." Her *Greek* series proved a big success and was featured in *Coilhouse Magazine*. J-Chan cites various influences, including Tim Burton, Colleen Atwood, the late Eiko Ishioka and the late Alexander McQueen; "It's their vision, married to amazing technique, which excites me." She likes to scout for rare fabrics from indie shops and to recycle old shower curtains, drapery and upholstery. Her favourite piece is one inspired by Tilda Swinton's performance in *Constantine*: "It's rather Elizabethan in conception." Of Steampunk she says "it will continue to evolve as long as artists bring new perspectives to it."

LEFT AND ABOVE:
Athena's Curse, Medusa's Fate.
Leather, lace knit, faux fur, vinyl, drapery sheer.

LEFT AND RIGHT:
Elizabethan Courtship. Vinyl,
upholstery, faux fur, taffeta, silk sari.

LEFT: *Elizabethan Courtship*. Vinyl, upholstery, faux fur, taffeta, silk sari.
ABOVE: *Athena's Curse, Medusa's Fate*. Vinyl, suede, knit, foil charmeuse, fishing net. Portrayed by Jessica Powell.

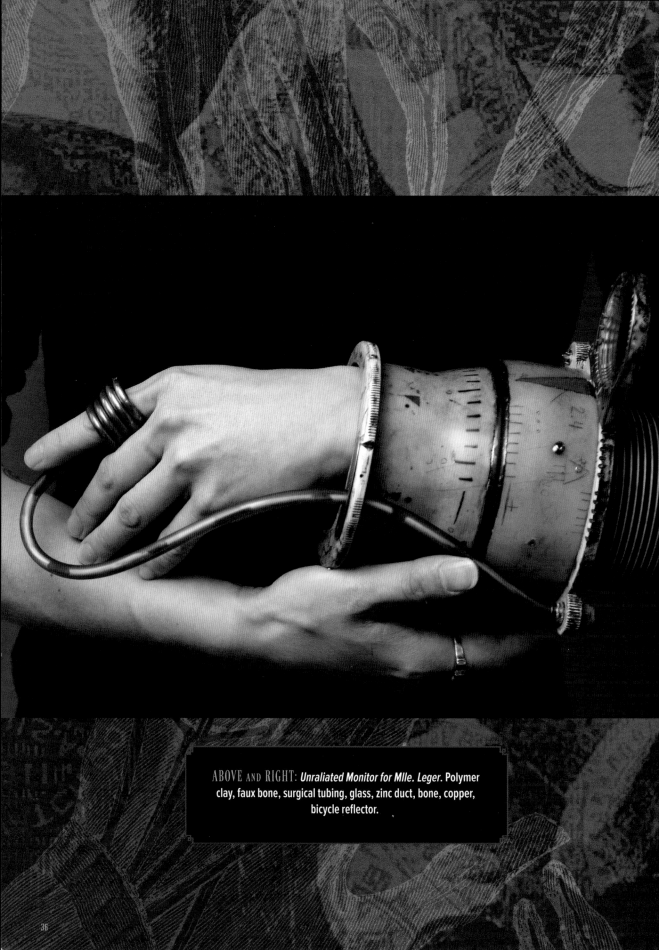

ABOVE AND RIGHT: *Unraliated Monitor for Mlle. Leger*. Polymer clay, faux bone, surgical tubing, glass, zinc duct, bone, copper, bicycle reflector.

"I was creating in my current vein for many years before I became aware of the Steampunk movement", says Robert, "I found it rather surprising, in fact, that my colleagues and I were considered to be Steampunk at all." Robert says that he does not try to make works that fit into the Steampunk genre, it's rather that objects he likes to create are so defined. His big influences, however, are firmly in the space – Jules Verne and the French silent film maker Georges Melies. He usually works on several pieces allied to the same narrative, in preparation for a museum or gallery show. The narrative will usually involve an invented character and time. One of his favourite pieces is his *Piperunulated Monitor for Mdme Duchamp*, made from panty hose stretched over an iron wire armature. "Unlike many Steampunk artists I like to fabricate my pieces to look like found objects; to me that adds a layer of meaning" he says. Robert has shown his work all over the world and many pieces are in gallery, museum and corporate collections in the US, Japan, the UK and Australia. He has also been published extensively, including in *Art Jewelry*, *Belle Armoire* and *Ornament* magazines. He thinks that Steampunk is here to stay: "It has become a fixture in the aesthetic landscape that defines our time. It will find its place in the chronicle of art history."

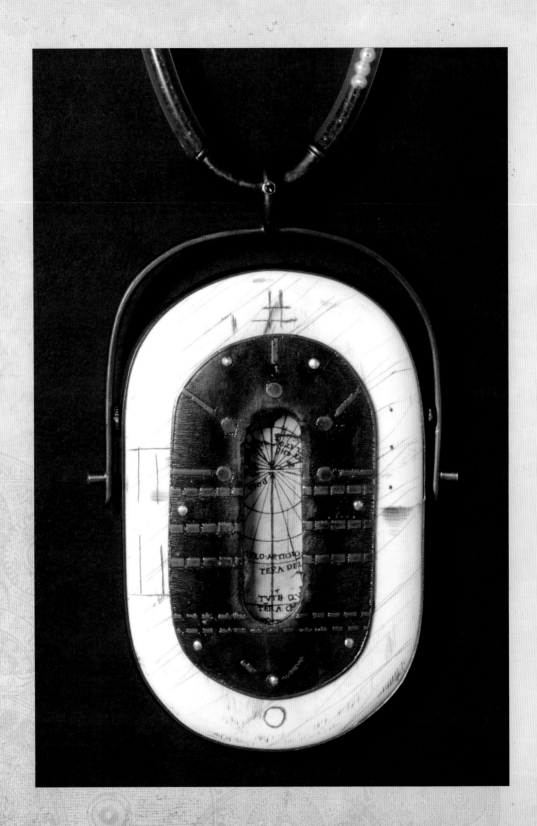

LEFT: *Thermo-Heliope Monitor.* Faux bone, etched copper, gemstones, sterling silver, surgical tubing, carborundum blasting sand.

BELOW: *Posianum Regulator for Mrs. Edison.* Electric range element, nylon membrane, polymer clay, etched copper, victrola sound head, pvc, surgical tubing.

ABOVE: *Lenamulation Monitor for Mme. Duchamp.* Faux bone, copper, brass, glass, surgical tubing, wood, paper, polymer clay, rubber, steel.

RIGHT: *Heart Monitor for Milan.* Faux bone, surgical tubing, copper, polymer clay, brass,

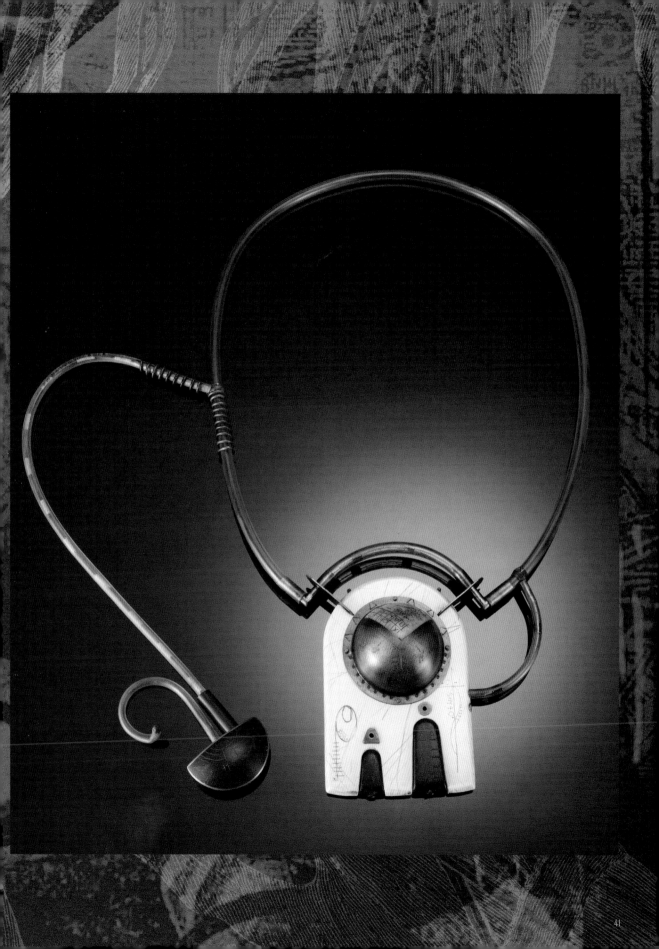

Dasowl was created by celebrated handbag designer Deborah S. Sciales (DAS) and Oliver W. Lowe (OWL), "on my return from Professor Calamity's famous exploration of the 'true' poles by dirigible", according to Oliver. Movies and theatre were the big influences, rather than other fashion designers, "films like *The Great Race* and endless episodes of *Masterpiece Theatre*." Self-taught ("Deborah studied under the Very Secret Order of Couturiers" and "Oliver was apprenticed to an undertaker, dressing bodies") they design what they would like to own and wear, using discontinued fabrics wherever possible. They've sold all over the world, most commissions coming via Etsy, and have noted different trends: "Camel hair spats sell really well in France, but not at all in Japan." Their clients – "mostly eccentrics" – include stilt walkers, aerial performers and musicians ("we hope the esteemed Thomas Dolby Esq. doesn't mind being mentioned") and they design for weddings and cosplay events. Dasowl are also fond of pre-Steampunk ('Clock-punk') and trace the roots of Steampunk back to Michael Moorcock's *Oswald Bastable* novels of the late '60s: "That's when a self-conscious retro-genre emerged, as opposed to the scientific romances of Jules Verne and H.G. Wells, but before the coining of the Steampunk term in the 1990s." They think the aesthetic will continue to flourish – "Steampunk is the high-water mark of civility, absurdity and innovative genius rolled into one."

LEFT: *Victorian Steampunk Bustle Skirt.* Silk, satin, lace.
ABOVE, LEFT: *Tapestry Bolero Skirt.* Silk. *Topper.* Red velvet, satin, brass.
ABOVE, RIGHT: *Swallowtail Steampunk Jacket.* Linen, lining in rayon and silk, brass buttons.

ABOVE: *Underbust Corset Belt.*
Burgundy leather, bone, cotton lining.
Polka Dot Victorian Bustle Skirt. Silk,
black satin, lace detail.
RIGHT: *Gentlemen's Steampunk Vest.*
Red velvet, silk, brass nautical buttons.
Provence Striped Trousers. Cotton
tapestry cloth.

"I may have been suffering from temporary insanity when I started my craft/fashion business" says Jane Faye, "I had no training, business experience or hyper-creative childhood. Two years later I get letters from happy customers; I guess looming bills do mean you pick up skills fast!" Jane Faye wasn't always into Steampunk, but loved upcycling, Victorian literature, costuming, feminism and "weird history." Then she met her partner, a founding member of the Glasgow Steampunk Society, and the spark was lit. Inspiration ? "Yes, it's hot gentlemen in goggles, and the attitude of alt. designers like Kambriel, Viona Lelegems and Fuschia of Stockingshock." She works with a small set of suppliers, like one Welsh family-owned business that only uses ethical, fair-trade and organic fabrics. "If only someone would bring Airship Freight into existance we could avoid shipping by CO_2 -spewing jet engines!" She sells a mix of made-to-order and unique items. Her favourite innovation is her secret compartment electric-blue bustle skirt: "storing your change in your behind is just downright funny." How about her working practices ? "Here in Glasgow we can't use fancy phrases like 'finding artistic flow' or 'creative energy', it's all about getting excited about an idea, then producing it to deadline!"

ABOVE: *Little Dark Riding Hood.* Black organic fairtrade velvet, vintage buttons, grey and black merino dreads, bamboo armwarmers.
LEFT: *Irene Bustle Skirt.* Vintage red velvet, recycled Re-P.E.T. duchess satin, merino Steampunk dreads, handmade braa dreadbeads, upcycled fishnet for sleeves.

LEFT AND ABOVE:
Secret Compartment Bustle Skirt.
Vintage brocade fabric, upcycled belt,
Eco-Fi felt mini hat, vintage jewelry
components.

"It all started when I was a kid", says Shawn Darling, a.k.a Gryphon's Egg, "when I began collecting Halloween masks. That led to mask-making for theatre and T.V.. I moved to work in L.A., at just about the time Steampunk was taking off, and I grabbed it." Gryphon's Egg is now well established as a favoured creator of costume accessories for Steampunk enthusiasts. His output consists almost entirely of froggles and gas masks, and he is an established member of the scene: "I even played in Vapor

Lock – a Steampunk band – for a while." He mostly works in latex rubber, "it's a material I know well as I've been creating with it for the past 25 years. I love its durability." Influences from his time in the Goth Industrial scene are still detectable, as are

other inspirations, including the artists Brom and H.R. Giger. He sells around the world, Australia, England and Canada in addition to the USA; many clients are in the movie or music scenes. Most buyers pick from his collection, although he does undertake rather more expensive commissions. Steampunk, he says, is in a healthy state, although "like many things it could grow from its small audience to become super-commercial, at which point all the life will be sucked out of it."

LEFT: *Froggle Skull Gas Mask.* **Latex construction.**
ABOVE: *Froggles (Frog Eye Goggles).* Latex construction, clear plastic lenses.

ABOVE: *Froggle Skull Combo.* Latex
construction.
RIGHT: *Standard Froggle Gas Mask.*
Latex construction with oxygen tubing.

FRISTON HO'OKANO

A 'retired' award-winning floral designer from Hawaii, Friston says that floral design and his interest in Steampunk can, and do, go together: "For over twenty years I tinkered with jewelry and vintage hardware as part of my floral creations. When Steampunk started breaking cover a few years back I offered some of these pieces on my Facebook page. Then demand went crazy and today I'm a full-time costume jewelry designer in the Steampunk style." Friston sees himself as providing the accessories that are an essential part of Steampunk fashion. He particularly likes pieces that use old moving clock parts: "my objective is to take pieces that are often iconic symbols of the 19th Century and use them to create an edgy but wearable art piece; each is like a floral composition, requiring movement, harmony and balance." Friston has received commissions from over 22 countries; his work is particularly popular in Australia and many clients are requesting pieces for Steampunk weddings. He no longer does conventions – "I just don't have time; keeping up with demand from my shop on Etsy is a full-time job in itself!"

ABOVE: Friston wearing *Steampunk Goggles*. Chrome welder goggles, plated brass gears, spinners, stamped figurals, magnifying glass loupe, vintage spoon handles, Swarovski crystals.

RIGHT: *Steampunk Time Traveller Ring*. Brass filigree ringband, oval brass cameo setting, brass wings, gold-plated pewter gear with brass spinner, copper Swarovski crystal.

LEFT, TOP: *Steampunk Lapel Pin.* Large brass gears, silver-plated filigree piece, pewter gear with Swarovski crystal.

LEFT, BOTTOM: *Persian Brooch.* Brass gears , stamped figurals, clockface image under glass cabochon, 12- and 18-gauge wire. Swarovski crystals.

ABOVE: *Medal of the Royal Order of Ganesha.* Layered brass figurals, filigree corner pieces, vintage button, Swarovski crystal.

LEFT: *Steampunk Wristband.* Dyed leather band, brass corner pieces, copper gear, brass gears and spinners, Swarovski crystal.

ABOVE: *Aviator Steam Ring.* Silver plated brass ringband. vintage timepiece, brass

Impero was created in 2006 by London College of Fashion graduate, Tilly and skilled tailor and leather specialist, Mumtaz. "From the start we wanted Impero to be a destination in London for avant garde leather tailoring. Our clothes are for those who want a look that's strong, elegant and above all individual," says Tilly. They are constantly re-inventing their style and visions for each new collection, revisiting fashions from the past and applying those designs and techniques in the present. "We do love luxurious textures and really refined leathers and like to think that great craftsmanship is also our signature." Their work is hugely influenced by Tim Burton. "His world is truly intoxicating, sending your imagination into overdrive. His scenes and characters are so loud and bright that he connects with a whole new layer of creativity," says Mumtaz, "we like to think we adopt a similar aesthetic in our work." With a loyal, influential and global clientele, which includes Oscar-winning movie stars, members of several royal families, musicians and fashion mavens, Impero have had massive plaudits, and their shop is recognized as a must-see destination in London for Steampunkers. Of Steampunk they say: "It's not a trend that will pass quickly; if anything the Steampunk revolution is only just getting started. Expect to see loads more Victorian-inspired fashion, film and music in the decade to come!"

LEFT: *Bolero (Ladies' coat).* Organic antiqued tan leather, black suede and lace trim. *Helmet and Bandoliers (Men's coat).* Hand-painted antique tan lamb's leather.
ABOVE: Impero's London shop.

ABOVE: *Alexander Jacket.* Handpainted midnight blue leather, with burgundy and navy suede trim.
RIGHT: *Bolero Jacket.* Organic, antiqued red leather, with black suede and lace trim.

RIGHT: *Bolero Jacket*. Organic, antiqued red leather, with black suede and lace trim.

ABOVE: *Admiral Coat.* Waterproof black nubuck, with gold piping.
RIGHT: *Demeter Ballgown.* Handpainted, multicoloured leather, decorated with hand-crafted leather roses.

LEFT and ABOVE:
2B Coat. Handpainted antique lamb's leather,
with decorative metal plates.

A mother and daughter (Sheridyn and Kaitlyn McClain) collaboration from "cold Minesota", KMK were driven by the need to create: "We painted, sculpted and sewed; the latter naturally led to costuming." As they became aware of Steampunk as a movement they found themselves creating in the style, "almost by osmosis: it's such a fun genre to play with." Inspired by Victorian designs, they have also drawn on Alexander McQueen, Vivienne Westwood, Japanese lolita fashion and '50s and '60s vintage. Everything is hand-made – "this helps us control quality and to create ethically" – silk dupinoi, cotton sateen, lace and taffeta are their favourite textiles. They love the fact they sell globally, "sometimes we pack for a client a mile away, then the next day it will be Sweden or Australia." Most work is for specific commissions, but sometimes a major Steampunk event, or the discovery of a new fabric will lead them to brainstorm and dream up something new for the sake of it. Their work has been extensively featured, including in *Dark Beauty*, *Guiseppina* and *Gothic Beauty* magazines, and on Alt Noir. About Steampunk as a movement they say "as long as it remains truly creative and fun, it will keep on growing."

LEFT AND ABOVE:
Dragonfly Desire Steampunk Wedding Gown. Silk damask and black satin.

ABOVE and RIGHT:
Military Steampunk Wedding Dress. Bronze polyester taffeta with red cotton and silk blend, tulle and cotton petticoat.

"I learnt to sew aged six from my mom, then dropped it until two years ago, when I created an 1880s-style dress for a convention; the biggest shock was realising how much fabric I needed for just one dress!" says Lisbeth Lovelloyd of Lady Love Lloyd. An interest in Victorian fashion meant that when she discovered Steampunk she was immediately attracted, "although the implied palette of greens, browns and greys can be limiting; I love all colours!" Inspiration comes from many sources, but particularly "manga and fantastic/ historic videogames. I also have a picture book from the Kyoto Fashion Institute by my bed." Amongst other Steampunkers she particularly admires Clockwork Couture, "their work is really impressive and so well made." Her main clients come from France; she usually works to commission, or "sometimes I just get the creative urge to make something for myself, then I become obsessive about fabrics and details." She thinks Steampunk is here to stay: "The aesthetic is more and more present in everyday life, in cartoons, music and design. I think it will grow into a significant lifestyle trend, rather like the Goth or Lolita movements."

LEFT: *Art-deco Shirt and Bustle Skirt.* Cotton, linen.
ABOVE: *Deep Blue and Hot Pink 1886.* Taffeta, satin, corsetry in cotton, steel bones, jersey.

LEFT, BELOW AND RIGHT:
The Ensemble Charbon. Cotton, black Lace, brown denim waistcoat with metallic gold buttons and cane.

"What we love about Steampunk is that it is not as rigidly defined as historical or film costuming; it really allows fertile and inventive minds to experiment and innovate", say owners Amy and Brayton Carpenter. Both natives of southern California with years of experience in historic costuming, they broadened their horizons in 2007, exhibiting at various pop culture conventions around the USA, which is how they came across the movement. "Jules Verne-inspired stuff had been around for a while, but as part of Steampunk it was somehow so much more potent, an aesthetic movement of like-minded artists with huge potential." Today their creations sell all over the world, and have been featured on ABC's *Castle* series, as well as in the *Steampunk: History Beyond Imagination* exhibition at the Muzeo in Anaheim, California. "We love playing with imaginary characters...." they say, ".....such as our Steampunk gladiator. We imagined him as a working-class man from 19th Century London.

He works in a dirigible factory, and at the end of the day goes straight from there to a seedy pub in Whitechapel. Donning armour and weapons, some from his daytime trade, he partakes in illegal games of bloody savagery, whilst the wealthy elite of London look on and gamble on the outcome." It is this power of imagination that has seen their other line of work – costuming - featured on many programmes o the History Channel, including *Mail Call*, *Soldiers for Hire* and *Jesse James*.

ABOVE: *Pub Gladiator Ensemble.* Skirting leather, 16-gauge sheet-brass, scavenged machine gears, upholstery leather, plastic face shield.

RIGHT: Steampunk medals, including *DSM Her Majesty's Mechanized Artillery* and *Badge of the Temple of Our Lady of Perpetual Motion*. Clock gears, jewelry and bead findings, gross-grain ribbon, re-purposed military buttons and insignia.

RIGHT: *Brayton and Amy's Expeditionary Attire.* Amy: Custom-made aviator cap, Aether sleeves, corset of russet leather, bustle skirt in copper/ black fabric; Brayton: Basic Victorian gentleman's ensemble, leather harness belt, sewn-on pistol scabbards, utility pouches, Aether sleeve, gators of chrome-tanned leather. Brass goggles by Chris Hornsby; rayguns by advanced-Light Weaponry.

LEFT: *Goggles.* Many examples transformed with metallic spray paints, gears, jewelet's loops, findings and "mad-cap whimsy".
BELOW: *Custom Holster for Ladies Steampunk Sidearm.* Tanned leather, lined with soft pig-suede, back panel with nautical theme "as a nod to Verne's *Nautilus* in *20,000 Leagues Under The Sea*".

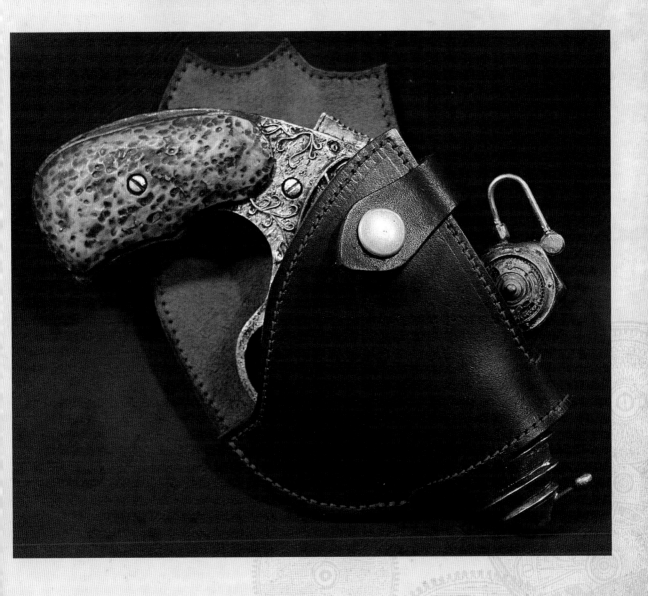

Marco Ribbe and Sina Collins started in business in 2001, with an alternative and medieval fashion store, "selling re-enactment apparel; being in the swim made us very aware of the emergence of Steampunk when it started happening in the US." Initially they observed the modding tradition, where you take ordinary objects and make them look Steampunk with Victorian-era fittings; "We always had a passion for the goth/Victorian age, so it struck a chord. However it took ages for the Steampunk thing to properly take root in Germany." They try not to observe what others are doing, so that they keep the originality and freshness of their ideas, so "movies and television – old cartoon series particularly – are the major sources of inspiration, together with museums and the vintage and found bits and pieces that we're surrounded with in our workshop." The workshop includes, in addition to the tailoring equipment, a kiln and lathe for creating original accessories. Marco is self-taught, whilst Sina, his fiancee, studies fashion design in Munich and models the clothes; they also employ a couple of professional tailors. Steampunk.de, their website, supplies the work of others in addition to their own; "Most of our work is individual pieces, although we will occasionally create a small collection, of corsages or headwear, for instance." Plans for the future include the imminent launch of the German *Steampunk Magazin*.

FAR LEFT: *Steampunk Starshooter.* Leather dress, fur trim and brass accessories.
LEFT: *Untitled.* Leather corset with brass rivets and miniature portrait panel, leather fascinator, Steampunk goggles, raygun.

FAR LEFT: *Phoenix.* Leather, fur, feathers, brass and clock parts fascinator, brass and leather Steampunk goggles.
LEFT: *Copper Girl.* Fabric, leather, brass rivets and roundels, brass and leather Steampunk goggles.

RIGHT: *The Golden Times.* Latex, gold leather platform boots, Steampunk goggles and blunderbuss.
FAR RIGHT: *We Own the Sky.* Leather corset, brass accessories, leather biker boots, Steampunk goggles, brass accessories.

LEFT: *Floating of Antlion.* Digital artwork.

RIGHT: *Spiral Memory.* Digital artwork.

92

Born in Hyoto, Japan, Kazuhiko Nakamura, a.k.a. Mechanical Mirage, a.k.a. Almacan, creates visions of what Steampunk wear might be: "My characters combine machine and body parts; miragic visions created with 3-D software. I love the freedom of expression that this software gives me, where the pixels construct something akin to a mirage in a desert." The influences are painting from Renaissance Northern Europe, Surrealism and Steampunk: "The impressions that these three soures create in my head turn into chemical connections in my brain." Now based in Kawasaki City, Japan, he thrives on juxtapositions: a surreal torture machine disguised as a vintage mannequin, influenced by the puppet movies of Jan Svankmajer and the Brothers Quay; a machine sculpture of Jeanne d'Arc is influenced by Hans Bellmer's sculptures; the treatment of a head is a vision of a mechanical pandora's box. The mastery of the software is impressive, and the visionary execution completely convincing: once you've seen one of his images they lodge in the memory. This is even more astonishing when one learns that this is not a full-time occupation; his day job is that of a designer. He has shown his work around the world, at *Asiagraph* in Tokyo, *Chimera* in Sedan, France, *Gravura do Douro*, Portugal, *Digital Palette* in Hartford CT, and at the *Terminus* show in Zurich. His work has also featured in numerous publications, including recently in *Steampunk: The Art of Victorian Futurism*.

ABOVE: *Triceratops.* Digital artwork.
RIGHT: *The End of Flight Zone.* Digital artwork.

LEFT: *Atoma*. Digital artwork.
ABOVE: *Automaton*. Digital artwork.

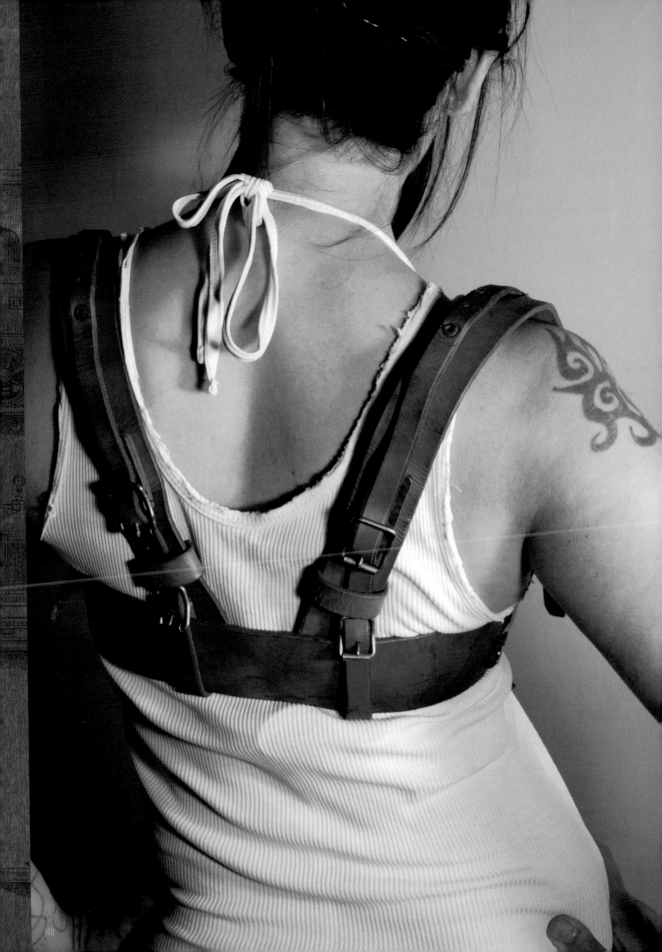

A collaboration between performer and designer, Paula Sana, and artist and photographer, Ronald Sulley, Vontoon was created in 2005. "Whilst working together on a number of photography projects, we both realised we shared an interest in the concept and design of movies like *At The Earth's Core*, *Master of the World* and *Captain Nemo and the Underwater City*", says Sana, "We were both passionate about technology, but were disappointed that we had been born too late to explore earth, too early to explore space". They began to explore

Steampunk aesthetics in some photographic work, then Sana began to use some items in her tribal fusion belly dances. When the latter took off – "we began to get commissions all over Scotland" – so did the clothes, and so they travelled with a stall. Bespoke commissions followed, and today most of their clients are in

the USA. Ms Vontoon make all their pieces with traditional tools; no machines are used at any point. "We use many different styles of leather so that each piece is as unique as possible. One signature of our style is 12-gauge spent shotgun cartridges: they make very handy containers." They also want to maintain a sense of subtlety and cool: "We want to create items that you can wear regularly, not just as part of a Steampunk outfit. For us Steampunk shouldn't be just cosplay or escapism, but a part of daily life."

LEFT: *Vintage Brace Set.* Leather, rivets, buckles.
ABOVE: *Yeti Hunter, With Vintage Brace Set and Belt.* Leather, rivets, buckles, spent cartridges, goggles.

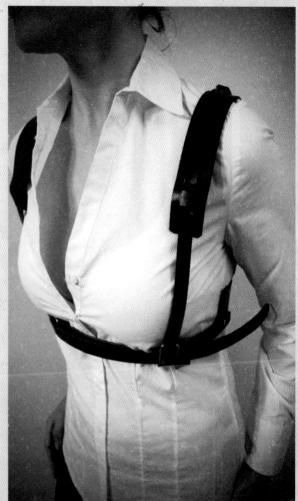

FAR LEFT: *Abbess Garter*. Leather, rivets, spent shotgun cartridges.
LEFT: *Toolers Brace Set*. Leather and buckles.
ABOVE: *Sky Pirate*. Cotton hyper crop top, vintage brace set, utility belt, leg holsters, spent shotgun cartridges.

LEFT: *Abbess Garter*. Leather, leather thonging, rivets, spent shotgun shells.
BELOW: *Jerryshop Boot Garter*. Leather, buckles, spent shotgun cartridges.

"I've always had an interest in strange, sci-fi, found objects, metal and handmade goods" says Deana Fukatsu of Octopus Me, "and cephalopods fit in with that; there's something so mysterious, evolved, alien and not-of-this-world about them. I saw my first octopus aged 20 in Mahaka and I'm still addicted to them.....their very existence inspires me." After training with Vasken Tanielan at the Rever Academy of Jewelry Arts in San Francisco, she apprenticed at his sudio for a year: "It was there that I discovered wax work, carving and casting...there's something so beautiful and primitive about it.....and I carried those techniques into my own jewelry practice." This she launched in 2007, just before she left for the Burning Man festival. Today she is well established in downtown San Francisco, producing octopus-inspired jewelry. She uses real octopus tentacles, casting in solid sterling silver, finishing with brushes and wheels. Sometimes she works with gold, using the same techniques, alloying the metal to the desired karat. The additional pieces in her creations are usually found objects, vintage or from a certified green source. She has clients from all over the world – USA, Russia, Europe, Singapore – including the sci-fi fantasy novelist China Meiville, and many collectors. She sells on Etsy and her new online store, as well as in galleries and at shows. Her work has been featured in the *Chicago Tribune* as well as on numerous blogs including *Stylehive*, *Steampunk Workshop* and *Trendhunter*.

LEFT FROM TOP: *Helix Tentacle Earrings, Tentacle Earrings, Octopus Sucker Plugs, Immortica Necklace, Wicked Tentacle Ring, Stacking Rings.* Oxidised Silver, blue diamond, rubies. ABOVE: *Immortica Necklace.* Oxidised silver.

LEFT AND ABOVE: *Kraken (Octopus Me and Miyu Decay Collaboration).* Oxidised silver with diamond.

LEFT FROM TOP: *Adorned Split Bangle, Crimson Earrings, Crimson Pendant*. Oxidised sterling silver, 18K yellow gold, rubies, red garnet.
ABOVE FROM TOP: *Tentacle Plugs, Enchanted Necklace, Rockstar Ring*. Oxidised sterling silver, diamond.

ABOVE: *For Amphitirite*, sterling silver.
RIGHT from top: *14K Yellow Gold Tentacle Ring, Cocktail Ring, Black Diamond Octopus Ring*, oxidised sterling silver, 14K gold, freshwater pearl, black diamond.

Based in Brazil and the US, Purpuratum is headed by Dr. Larissa H. Haut, who holds a PhD in Biotechnology. "I did play the part of the intrepid steampunk explorer in the Brazilian rainforest as part of my research, but I really came to Steampunk via an interest in period-accurate clothing." Coming from a long line of fashion designers and seamstresses, Larissa sees connections between fashion and science: "Both force us to ask questions about who we are and our environment; both involve ideas translated into concepts which are then tested and brought to life, by hand and mind working in unison." Purpuratum work almost exclusively to commission, when the project and the people are of interest. "We don't design our pieces as individual items, but as full outfits that represent an individual character, with their aspirations, needs and social context. The same process applies whether they are a privateer, antiquarian or adventurous naturalist." Sources of inspiration include Vionnet, Dior, Alexander McQueen and, of course, Steampunk itself. "The scene is a wonderful environment where several sub-cultures can collide to beget something new and provocative; we hope to continue to be part of its growth and evolution."

LEFT AND ABOVE: *Countess Isabela della-Cord, Archaeological Explorer.* Brass, copper, leather, satin, silk.
RIGHT: Dr. Larissa H. Haut.

ABOVE and RIGHT:
*Doctor Gwendolen Bessworth,
Naturalist and Paleontologist.* Brass,
cotton, feather, fur, leather, voile.

FAR LEFT: *Margaretha Delluva Palantine, Spymaster.* Chamois, lace, passementerie, satin, sequin, silk, velvet, voile.
ABOVE: *Jeanne Antoinette Poisson, Marquise de Pompadour.* Feather, glass beads, leather, passementerie, satin, taffeta, velvet.

LEFT: *Susanna von Slayer,*
Renegade Automaton Disposaler.
Brass, fur, lace, leather,
passementerie, taffeta, silk
fringe .
ABOVE: *Margaretha Delluva*
Palantine, Spymaster.
Chamois, fur, lace,
passementerie, satin, silk, velvet,
voile.

Skinz 'N' Hydez

Ian Finch-Field grew up in an artistic family, making, creating and dismantling since he was a young lad; "I always had a fascination with how things worked, especially electronics....add to that an obsession with medieval armour and weaponry, mix in an almost religious love of sci-fi/post apocalyptic movies and you have my style!" He stumbled on Steampunk by accident: "I created a bracer, posted it online and back came loads of responses telling me it was really Steampunk, so I just carried on." He sees himself as a creator of wearable art for the Steampunk movement, always well-crafted as well as brilliantly creative. Inspiration comes from many sources, not least his wife Christy Johnson of Christys Jewelry, Tom Banwell and Bob Bassett. Creating is the easy bit; "I have a vague idea in my head, start working out the patterns to make it and see it come alive as I shape and mould." The hard part was establishing himself and keeping the business growing. Now highly collectable (one client, Sky Captain Gannon, has thirty pieces and counting; Daniel Proulx, with whom he has worked is another), Finch-Field sells mainly in the UK and US. His work has been extensively featured, including in *Cosplay Gen*, *Pegasus* and famously in Justin Bieber's video of *Santa Claus Is Coming To Town*.

LEFT: *Steampunk Gauntlet*. Cowhide leather, rivets and studs , LED lights, found vintage objects.
ABOVE: *Justin Bieber's Steampunk Robot* (still from the music video *Santa Claus is Coming to Town*). Cowhide leather, brass sheet, rivets and studs, LED lights, vintage pocket watch and found objects.

BELOW: *Emperor's Armor of Empowerment.* Cowhide leather, brass sheet, rivets and studs, LED lights, vintage parts.

FAR RIGHT: *Steampunk Mechanical Spider Bracer.* Collaboration with Daniel Proulx of Catherinette Rings. Cowhide leather, brass sheet, rivets and studs, copper wire, clock movement and cogs.

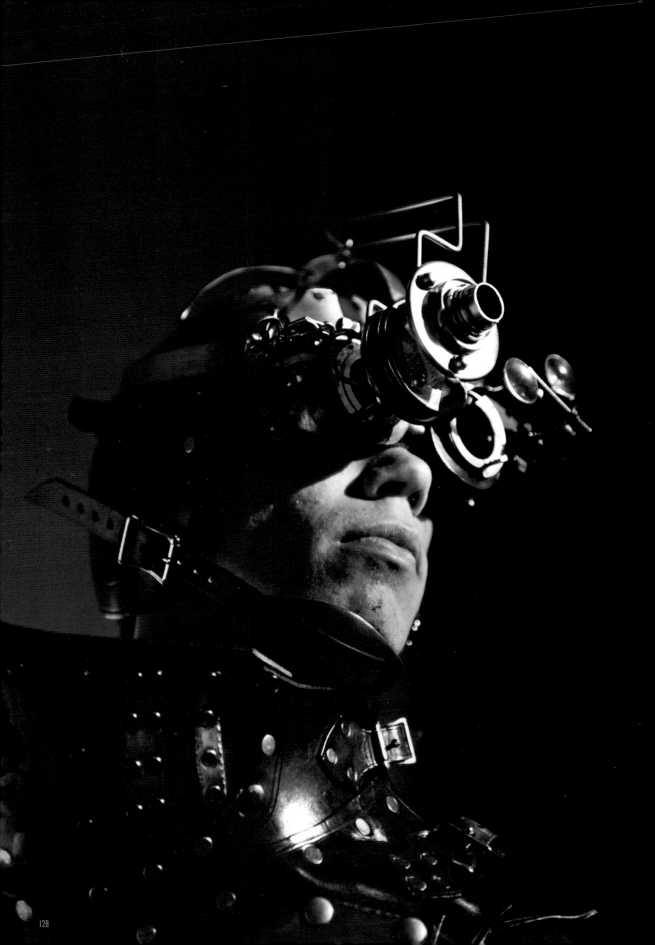

LEFT: *Traveller of Time*. Goggles: Cowhide leather, brass sheet, rivets and studs, found objects, lenses. Body armour: Cowhide leather.

ABOVE: *Steampunk Rocketeer Backback*. Cowhide leather, brass sheet, rivets and studs, vintage fire extinguisher, vintage found objects.

STEAMPUNK COUTURE

"I'd been designing for years before I started Steampunk Couture. As I was there as the movement was in its infancy, it was a natural move" says Kato of the genesis of her business. Her best ideas come "in the middle of the night. I keep a notepad by my bed specifically to jot the 2 a.m. ideas down. They aren't really from a particular source, it's more like 99% inspiration." Keeping her signature style fresh and inventive means consciously not looking at what other designers in the genre are doing. It does mean regular trips to L.A. 's fashion district

to look for new and striking fabrics, trim and buttons. Kato never studied fashion, but did do a nine month art course in Wales, which although it included a fashion and textile module "didn't really offer any guidance. I taught myself everything and that's my greatest personal achievement." She sells all over the world: "South Africa, the Cayman Islands, Germany, Italy and of course the US. Most of my clients are women. Quite a few

are wonderful collectors who snap up my pieces within 60 seconds of their online release!" Her main problem is meeting customer demand; she turns down magazine exposure regularly, as well as fashion shows – "it's genuinely that I don't have the time" – although amongst those who have got through to feature her work include *Elle, SFX, Gothic Lifestyle, Hustler, Bizarre, Gothic Beauty, FAE* and *curve Curve.* She thinks Steampunk will last "a good handsomely long time, just as Goth and Punk did."

LEFT: *Apocalypse Girl.* Faux leather jacket, faux leather belt harness, thigh-highs, leather belt, Steampunk goggles.
ABOVE: *Headdress.* Leather and brass.

FAR LEFT AND BELOW: *Cadet Connie.* Faux leather jacket, Steampunk Blunderbuss, with brass sights, black and brown Steam pants.
LEFT: *Headphones.* Leather and brass.

LEFT: *Military Red Riding Hood.* Military-inspired red wool coat, underbust *Ryonen* corset, Steampunk goggles.
ABOVE: *White Steam Full Outfit.* Stretch, lace-covered white bib top, vintage pearlescent button detail, vintage bridal skirt, white wig.

LEFT: *The Governess.* Stretch velvet, satin layer bustle, satin cravat, vintage pewter buttons.
ABOVE: *Gearwerks Outfit.* Cotton with velvet detailing and pearl buttons.

LEFT: *Lady Genevieve*. Cotton, brocade and lace.
ABOVE: *Striped Playsuit and Buckles*. Leather, lace, poly cotton, raw cotton and brass.

ABOVE: *Jailer's Wife*. Serge cotton, bone buttons, brass girdle with vintage keys.
RIGHT: *Lady Winter*. Cotton, faux leather felt, suede thigh-high boots.

Liam Brandon Murray, a.k.a The Steampunk Overlord, came to Steampunk via Cosplay: "I had always been a creative being and when I stumbled on cosplay, I saw a way of expressing myself artistically." He works "almost entirely from my imagination", trying to avoid direct influences. Each costume takes a long time to dream up, sometimes up to a year. Whilst the creative process is personal, the build involves a team of talents: "I really want to recognise those who help me; as we're doing new things, it involves a huge amount of patience." For Liam,

Steampunk is a reflection of a Victorian zeal for invention and craftsmanship. "It's amazing what's happened to the movement and how Hollywood and quite a few pop bands have tapped into it.... it makes you wonder where else it can go....maybe we need a new cosplay genre, LOL." To this end Liam has dreamt up his own new genre – Cirquepunk or Circus Punk. "I hope it will be the next

big costume movement; it's got huge potential when you think of how one can fuse the different circus traditions from different acts and decades." He feels strongly that cosplay can be an art form and wants to distinguish between people who dabble and those who create with his intensity. "We need a new term, maybe Cospro, to identify those who are taking it to a new level. I have respect for anyone doing it on any level, including those who treat it as just a hobby, but it would be good to also recognise and promote the artists in the culture."

LEFT: *Cirque Punk*. Latex, leather, resin, paint.
ABOVE: *Steampunk Overlord and his Wing Commander*. Leather, brass, plyboard, resin, plastic

LEFT: *Cirquepunk/ Steam*. Materials used: "too many to mention!"
ABOVE: *Overlord Meets the Mad Hatter*. Leather, latex, brass.

ABOVE AND RIGHT:
Icarus Wings I. Black walnut, cherry, maple, arbutus and mahogany with repurposed vintage gauges and pulleys; leather straps and nylon cord.

Based on Vancouver Island, British Columbia, Kyle originally trained as a cabinet maker, but started taking an interest in his spare time in projects that were "rather more unusual", creating a workshop at home for the purpose. One of his first creations was a pair of wooden wings for his wife to wear to the Victoria B.C. Steampunk Exhibition. These became the prototypes for Thin Gypsy Thief's signature *Icarus Wings*. Many pieces later, Kyle stills finds inspiration from "making things that I can't find otherwise. Similarly I will get ideas from seeing something in a movie or videogame, a piece of fantasy that has come from the mind of an artist or film-maker, and I will try and make it a reality; that process is really inspiring and fun." Fellow Steampunkers also feature in those sources which spark creativity, including the custom lightwork of Art Donovan, the metalwork of Eric Freitas, the leatherwork of Ian Finchfield and the clothes by Steampunk Couture. "The Steampunk community is full of overwhelmingly positive aficionados and mutually-supporting artists. Social media has been a huge part of this." Kyle's clients come from Europe, Japan, Australia and China as well as the USA. He notably created a pair of steampunk microphones ("one very Steampunk, the other a bit more Mad Max") for two-times grammy-winner, T-Pain.

ABOVE AND RIGHT:
Icarus Wings II. Black walnut, cherry, maple, arbutus and
mahogany with repurposed vintage gauges and pulleys;
leather straps and nylon cord.

LEFT: *Steampunk Bass.* Cherry and maple woods, custom made brass gauges.
ABOVE: *T-Pain Steampunk Microphone.* Black walnut, maple, brass, glass, lighting effects.

LEFT, TOP: *Headphones*. Black walnut, maple, brass, leather.
LEFT, BELOW: *Vaporiser*. Black walnut, maple, birch, velvet, glass and brass.
RIGHT AND BELOW: *Steampunk Guitar*. Vintage electric guitar, black walnut, brass, antique typewriter parts.

ABOVE and LEFT:
Steampunk Goggles. Plastic, acrylic,
glass, copper, brass and leather.

APPENDIX

Designers' Contact Details

Tom Banwell	tombanwell.etsy.com
Dr. Brassy Steamington	DrBrassysSteampunk.etsy.com
J-Chan Designs	jchansdesigns.com
Robert Dancik	fauxbone.com
Dasowl	facebook.com/dasowlclothing
Gaia Noir	GaiaNoir.etsy.com
Gryphon's Egg	gryphoneggproductions.com
Friston Ho'okano	DesignsByFriston.etsy.com
Impero London	imperolondon.co.uk
KMK Designs	kmkdesigns.org
Lady Love Lloyd	ladylovelloyd.etsy.com
Legendary Costume Works	legendarycostumeworks.com
Lost Legends	lostlegends.de
Mechanical Mirage	mechanicalmirage.com
Ms Vontoon	msvontoon.co.uk
Octopus Me	octopusmejewelry.com
Purpuratum	Purpuratum.etsy.com
Skinz 'N' Hydez	skinznhydez.etsy.com
Steampunk Couture	steampunkcouture.com
Steampunk Overlord	steampunkoverlord.deviantart.com
Thin Gypsy Thief	thingypsythief.com

CREDITS

p. 8, p.9, p.12, p.13, p.14, p.15, p.17,
p.18, p.19:
Photography by Topher Adam.

p.10, p.11, p.16:
Photography by Tom Banwell.

p. 30, p. 31:
Character portrayed by Elizabeth
Maiden.
Photography by Nina Pak.

p.32, p.33, p.34:
Models - Josephine Silverwolf &
Elizabeth Maiden.
Photography by Nina Pak.

p.35:
Character portrayed by Jessica Rowell
of J-Chan's Designs.
Photography by Nina Pak.

p.46:
Photography by Stuart Crawford.
Modelled by Helen Beaumont .

p.47:
Photography by Duncan Holmes.
Modelled by Jane Faye.

p.48, p.49, p.50:
Photography by Graham Ritchie.
Modelled by Raven Ember.
Hair by Peter Mellon.

p. 60:
Photography by Martin Small of
Soulstealer Photography.

p.64 - 65:
Photography by Hilde Kvivik Kavli.

p. 70, p.71:
Photography by Fairshadow
Photography.
Modelled by Edith.
Hair by Amber Rose.
Make-up by Lucinda Connaker at
Being Fab.

p. 72, p.73:
Photography by Photosynthetique.
Modelled by Lady Rose Hips.

p.86, p.87, p.89, p.90, p91:
Photograpby by Marco Ribbe.

p.106:
Photography by Allan Amato.
Modelled by Ulorin Vex.
Clothing by S & G Clothing.

p. 110
Photography by Allan Amato.
Modelled by Alexandra Matthews.
Clothing by S & G Clothing.

p. 111
Photography by Allan Amato.
Modelled by Chris Jackson.
Clothing by S & G Clothing.

p.114, p.115, p.116, p.117, p.121, p.123:
Photography by Jerry Bennett /
jerrybennettphoto.com.
Make-up and Hair by Julianne Ulrich /
julianneulrich.com
Modelled by Jordana Jagdeo.
Stylists - Larissa Herkenhoff Haut and
Trevor Hughes.

p.118, p.119, p.122:
Photography by Primo Tacca Neto /
tacca.com.br.
Make-up and Hair by Melissa
Trierweiler.
Modelled by Pamela Eloise Herkenhoff
and Aline da Silva.
Stylists - Larissa Herkenhoff Haut and
Renata Tacca.

p.124, p.127:
Photography by Daniel Proulx.

p.128:
Photography by Jen Steele.

p.129:
Photography by Jerome Lin.

p.148, p.149, p.154, p.155:
Photography by Alysia Miller.

p.150, p.151, p.152, p.156, p.157:
Photography by Winterwolf Studios.

p.153:
Photography by Terry Soo /
SoulbridgeMedia.com.